LIFE CYCLE OF A

HONEYBEE

By Kirsty Holmes

KidHaven
PUBLISHING

Words that look like **this** can be found in the glossary on page 24.

Published in 2019 by
KidHaven Publishing, an Imprint of Greenhaven Publishing, LLC
353 3rd Avenue, Suite 255, New York, NY 10010

© 2019 Booklife Publishing

This edition is published by arrangement with Booklife Publishing.

Designer: Daniel Scase
Editor: Holly Duhig

Cataloging-in-Publication Data

Names: Holmes, Kirsty.
Title: Life cycle of a honeybee / Kirsty Holmes.
Description: New York : KidHaven Publishing, 2019. | Series: Life cycles | Includes glossary and index.
Identifiers: ISBN 9781534527287 (pbk.) | 9781534527270 (library bound) | ISBN 9781534527294 (6 pack) | ISBN 9781534527300 (ebook)
Subjects: LCSH: Honeybee--Life cycles--Juvenile literature. | Honeybee--Juvenile literature.
Classification: LCC QL568.A6 H65 2019 | DDC 595.79'9--dc23

Printed in the United States of America

Please visit our website, www.greenhavenpublishing.com. For a free color catalog of all our high-quality books, call toll free 1-844-317-7404 or fax 1-844-317-7405.

CPSIA compliance information: Batch # BS18KL : For further information contact Greenhaven Publishing LLC, New York, New York at 1-844-317-7404.

PHOTO CREDITS
Photocredits: Abbreviations: l-left, r-right, b-bottom, t-top, c-center, m-middle.
Front Cover – Hintau Aliaksei, bg – perlphoto. 1m – Hintau Aliaksei, bg – perlphoto. 3 – Linus T. 3bg – perlphoto, 3tr – DJTaylor, 3mr – bluecrayola, 3br – davemhuntphotography. 4l – Oksana Kuzmina, 4m – Dmitry Lobanov, 4r – Pressmaster. 5l – Alliance, 5m – Elnur, 5r – Josep Curto. 6 – Rudmer Zwerver. 7 – Aleksey Stemmer. 8 – Roy Pederson. 9 – Ian Grainger. 10 – vvoe. 11 – Dr Morley Read. 12 – Jay Ondreicka. 13 – kungfoofoto. 14 – Freebilly. 15 – davemhuntphotography. 16 – Krisda Ponchaipulltawee. 17 – Cathy Keifer. 18tl – reptiles4all, 18br – Dirk Ercken. 19tr – Ficmajstr, 19br – Rudmer Zwerver. 20 – Mircea C. 21 – Choke29. 22l – Peter Baxter. 22m – Edvard Mizsei 22-23m – Steve Byland. 23m – Daniele Carotenuto. 23r – Gerald A. DeBoer.
Images are courtesy of Shutterstock.com. With thanks to Getty Images, Thinkstock Photo and iStockphoto

WHAT IS A LIFE CYCLE?

All living things have a life cycle. They are all born, they all grow bigger, and their bodies change.

Child

Baby

Toddler

When they are fully grown, they have **offspring** of their own. In the end, all living things die. This is the life cycle.

Teenager

Adult

Elderly Person

HELPFUL HONEYBEES

Honeybees are flying insects. They have two wings and yellow-and-black stripy bodies. They have six legs and a special long feeding tube, called a proboscis.

Wings

Proboscis

Worker bees have a sting in their tail – but they will die if they use it.

Legs

There can be up to 80,000 honeybees in a colony!

Bees live in large groups, called colonies, in a special home, called a hive. There are three types of honeybee in a colony: a drone (male) bee, a worker (female) bee, and one female queen bee.

EXCELLENT EGGS

Honeybees make a special wax, called beeswax. They use this to build lots of little **hexagons**, called honeycomb. This is the perfect place for honeybee eggs to be kept safe.

The eggs look like grains of rice, and are stuck to the honeycomb with sticky **mucus**.

Eggs

Only the queen bee in a honeybee colony can lay eggs. She lays her eggs in the spring. She can lay up to 1,500 eggs in a single day!

LITTLE LARVAE

Bee Larva

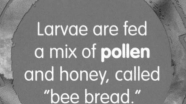

Larvae are fed a mix of **pollen** and honey, called "bee bread."

After three days, the eggs hatch into **larvae**. Worker bees have the special job of feeding the larvae. Each larva is fed 1,300 times a day.

Larvae that will be queens one day are fed a special food called "royal jelly." This helps those larvae grow bigger than the others, and become young queens.

Royal Jelly

Larvae have no legs, eyes, **antennae** or wings – just a tiny mouth.

PATIENT PUPAE

Sealed
Honeycomb
Cells

After about six days, the workers and drones seal up the cells with wax. Once they are sealed in, the larvae will spin a **cocoon** around their bodies. Each larva is now a pupa.

Inside the cocoon, the pupa is changing fast. It develops eyes, legs, and wings. It grows tiny hairs and gets its black-and-yellow stripes.

The honeybee chews its way out of the cocoon when it's ready.

HAPPY HONEYBEES

A colony of honeybees could have 60,000 worker bees, 600 drone bees, and one queen. Some bees live in hives in the wild, while others live in man-made hives.

People who keep hives are called beekeepers.

Worker bees collect pollen and **nectar** from flowers. They turn the nectar into honey, which they eat and feed to larvae – and which humans like to eat, too!

LIFE AS A HONEYBEE

Worker bees are all female. Their job is to gather food, clean the cells, feed larvae, and look after the queen. They also guard the hive and build new cells.

A drone bee's only job is to **mate** with a queen bee, so she can have offspring. Once the drone bee has mated with a queen, the drone bee dies.

Queen Bee

Drone Bees

Queen bees lay eggs. They only leave the hive to mate, or to begin a new colony somewhere else.

FUN FACTS ABOUT HONEYBEES

Bees are the only insect to produce a food that humans like to eat.

- **Honeybees have been around for millions of years.**

- Bees tell each other where nectar can be found by dancing!

- **Honeybees do not have eyelids, and can't close their eyes.**

- Honeybees have two stomachs; one for their own food, and one to store nectar to make honey.

- Honeybee wings flap at about 200 beats per second. This is what makes bees buzz!

Drone bees live for about 90 days, and die as soon as they mate with a queen. Worker bees live for about 40 days. Queens can live up to four years.

Honeybees are at risk from **climate change**. It is important to protect bees because they help us grow plants to eat.

If you see a bee on the ground, try giving it a teaspoon of sugary water to sip.

THE LIFE CYCLE

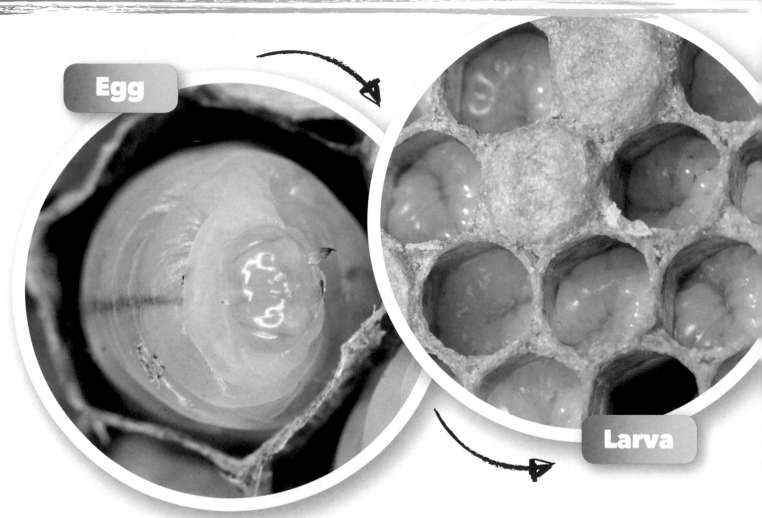

Egg

Larva

The life cycle of a honeybee has different stages.
All the stages are different.

Adult

Emerging Honeybee

The honeybee egg grows into a larva. The larva becomes a pupa, then an adult. Adult drones and queens produce offspring and workers help the hive.

In the end, the bee dies, and the life cycle is complete.

GLOSSARY

antennae	a pair of long, thin sensors found on the heads of insects
climate change	a change in the typical weather or temperature of a large area
cocoon	a silky case spun by the larvae of many insects for protection as they change into their adult form
hexagons	six-sided shapes
larvae	young insects that must grow and change before they can reach their adult form
mate	to produce young with an animal of the same species
mucus	a thick liquid that is produced in some parts of an animal's body
nectar	a sweet liquid made by flowers in order to attract insects
offspring	the child, or young, of a living thing
pollen	a powder-like substance made by plants

INDEX